Original title:
Island Rays

Copyright © 2025 Creative Arts Management OÜ
All rights reserved.

Author: Aidan Marlowe
ISBN HARDBACK: 978-1-80581-675-1
ISBN PAPERBACK: 978-1-80581-202-9
ISBN EBOOK: 978-1-80581-675-1

Sunlit Shores

The seagulls squawk and flap, so bold,
They steal my fries, or so I'm told.
I toss a chip, they dive like thieves,
While I just laugh, and plot my leaves.

The sunbeam slips into my drink,
With every sip, I start to think.
In shades so big, I lose my feet,
And dance with crabs, quite incomplete.

Echoes of Coastal Bliss

I prance along the sandy path,
With jellyfish, I share a laugh.
They jiggle close, I leap and scream,
Who knew that sea could be a dream?

The waves bring secrets, fine and neat,
From fish who gossip with their feet.
I can't keep up, I twist and twirl,
While starfish giggle, give a whirl.

Light Dancing on Water

Bright beams waltz across the waves,
I spin with dolphins, oh how brave!
But one mischievous little fluke
Bumped me hard, and now I'm loose.

The sun's a disco, shining bright,
With every splish, I lose the fight.
I slip and slide down sandy slopes,
While seaweed strikes, just like I hoped!

Serene Haven of Solitude

In my cocoon of solitude,
A crab appeared, so crude, so rude.
I shared my snacks, he called me names,
While nearby gulls cheered for the games.

A soft breeze tickles my bare toes,
Whispers of laughter follow close.
In stillness wrapped, I hear their cheer,
As they're all up to something near!

Shoreline Serenity

Seagulls squawk and steal my fries,
A crab scuttles by, oh how it tries.
Sand gets in places, not meant to be,
I dance like a fool, oh look at me!

A Glimpse of Paradise

The sun's like a pancake, golden and round,
In flip-flops, I tumble, then tumble, I sound.
Palm trees are swaying, they're having a blast,
I'm chasing my drink, oh how long will it last?

Warmth Beneath the Palms

Bikini tops fly like kites in the breeze,
A picnic of snacks, just trying to please.
Sandy dogs shake, and it's chaos galore,
The old folks are sunbathing, can't take anymore!

Celestial Beachcomber

Shells like treasure, I'm on a quest,
Each one I find, I think I'm the best.
A flip-flop disaster, they're lost in the sea,
I wave at the waves, they wave back at me!

Serenity in Sunbeams

A seagull stole my sandwich today,
I laughed as it squawked and flew away.
Chillin' on sand with my toes out,
Wishing for waves, not a pesky shout.

The sun paints my nose a lovely shade,
I tried to stay still, but then I strayed.
With kids running wild and a dog who sways,
I guess I'll just bask in these wild displays.

Calm Waters and Brilliant Skies

My boat's a bit leakier than I planned,
But who needs dry while I'm on this strand?
I paddled with flair, how'd I end up wet?
Laughing at the clouds, can't have regrets yet.

Fish splash around, making such a scene,
I snorkel for treasure, find only green beans.
My sunscreen is strong, it smells like a mix,
Of vacation dreams and some sunscreen tricks.

Horizon's Embrace

Chasing the sunset, I lost my flip-flop,
The waves chewed it up; oh well, no stop!
The horizon whispers tales I can't hear,
But I'll still pretend it's a job I hold dear.

A crab in a tux splashed a drink on my knee,
I swear it just winked, what a sight to see!
With laughter abound and a dance on the shore,
I'm king of the beach, what could I ask for?

Golden Hours on the Sea

Sunset cocktails served with a twist,
The bartender's tips got me quite the list.
I'm sipping with style, or maybe a spill,
Sunshine and laughter, oh what a thrill!

The waves crash in rhythm, a musical beat,
I jiggle and wiggle, all twinkly and sweet.
Was that a fish joke, or did I just dream?
No worries on this trip; I'm lighting the beam!

Radiance of the Retreat

In the sun, I found my flip-flops,
Dancing with the crabs in flip-flops.
Seagulls squawking, a comedic flock,
Chasing my sandwich, oh what a shock!

Palm trees laughing with breezy glee,
Swaying as if they share my spree.
Lemonade spills on my sunburned nose,
The joy of chaos, it only grows!

Bees buzzing fiercely, oh what a buzz,
Humming to the scent of melted fuzz.
A hammock swings as if it knows,
Life's a giggle in bright summer clothes!

Elysian Shoreline

Oh, the waves, they prance and play,
Like toddlers on a summer day.
I build a castle, it stands so tall,
Then a wave giggles, and down it falls!

A fishy friend tried to steal my bait,
A tug-of-war, it was a debate.
But who could resist such silly fun,
When sun-kissed laughter is never done?

My sunscreen's on, or is it pie?
It's hard to tell, oh my, oh my!
With laughter echoing on the shore,
I find myself wishing for more!

A Symphony of Solace

Turtles glide by with a casual flair,
Winking at me as if unaware.
I play my ukulele, a tune so fine,
But a crab joins in, claiming it's mine!

Seashells gossip, with whispers so bright,
They chat of the tides and moonlight sprites.
I shuffle my feet, making them dance,
The ocean chuckles, oh what a chance!

A pelican swoops for a snack, oh dear,
Sharing my chips without any fear.
In this zany serenade of sun,
Life's a concert of laughter and fun!

Whispers of the Deep

Bubbles rise like giggles, amused,
A school of fish, all confused.
They dart around, like kids at play,
While I just want to float away.

Octopus jests with a wink and grin,
Slinging seaweed; tricky to win.
My snorkel's crooked, I can't quite breathe,
A mermaid laughs, "Just take your leave!"

The sun dips low, colors all a-mish,
I wave to dolphins, they're doing the swish.
As night falls down, shadows in fun,
The ocean's a party, never done!

Vestiges of the Ocean

The crab did a jig, all sideways and quick,
Said, 'Look at my moves!' while doing a flick.
A starfish chimed in, 'I can stretch 'til I burst!'
As the clams whispered gossip, they quarreled and cursed.

A seagull dropped fries, oh what a display,
While dolphins rolled in, making a splash play.
The fish wore their glasses and danced in a line,
While the seaweed just laughed, 'Oh, isn't this fine?'

Gentle Caress of Seafoam

The waves tickled toes, what a silly delight,
As beach balls flew past in a colorful flight.
A jellyfish giggled while floating about,
Saying, 'I'd love to join, but I'm still stuck in doubt!'

The sandcastles wobbled, like they drank too much sprite,

While children giggled, running left and then right.
A sunburnt old crab just rolled his eyes wide,
'You young ones are wild; I'm just here for the tide!'

Windswept Bliss

The kites soared up high, with tails full of cheer,
While the wind whispered secrets for all to hear.
A parrot exclaimed, 'What a lovely hat!'
As a friend with a bucket just said, 'What's that?'

The breeze played its tune, like a comical band,
While flip-flops would flop, like they couldn't quite stand.

A crab choreographed moves to the sound,
While the surf brought the laughs, gaily swirling around.

Prisms on the Sand

The sun winked down, painting colors so bright,
While beachgoers laughed till they fell in delight.
A turtle tried surfing, just flopped with a plop,
As seagulls all chuckled, 'When will he stop?'

The shells held a meeting, discussing their fate,
'To shine and get picked, or to just sit and wait?'
With each wave that came, they sparkled and swayed,
As laughter and joy filled the scenes that were laid.

Radiant Reflections

In the mirror of the sea,
Fish flash smiles, can't you see?
Waves giggle in a playful dance,
Even crabs join in with a prance.

Seagulls squawk with flair and jest,
Wearing sunglasses at their best.
They dive for fries we left behind,
Seeking snacks, they're quite unconfined.

Palm trees sway, they can't be shy,
Bending low to wave goodbye.
Each sunbeam wears a jaunty hat,
While turtles wink and chat like that.

Laughter echoes off the shore,
Sandcastles built, then crushed once more.
Underneath the playful rays,
We find joy in silly ways.

Whispering Tides

The water whispers tales of cheer,
With a splash, we draw it near.
Sea foam tickles toes and feets,
Chasing crabs, oh what a treat!

Tiny fish form a merry band,
Singing songs of the silly sand.
Melodies ride on the breezy air,
While the shells giggle without a care.

We float along, with lemonade in hand,
Watching jellyfish doing the stand.
Octopus juggling shells with glee,
Underwater circus, come and see!

As the tide rolls in for a peek,
Seashells wear hats, so unique.
With every wave, a new surprise,
As laughter dances under the skies.

Golden Horizon Dreams

In golden hues, the sun will laugh,
Dancing lightly like a giraffe.
Clouds wear bow ties, oh so fine,
As we sip on tropical wine.

Flip-flops flopping, we strut with pride,
While the beach ball takes a ride.
Sunburns happen, we all agree,
Like lobsters in a comedy spree.

Surfers wipe out, but don't you fret,
They rise again, no hint of regret.
The ocean giggles, waves take a shot,
In this play, we're all a lot!

Dreams of coconuts and fun galore,
With every sunset, we want more.
Underneath this brightening glow,
Life's a joke, come on, let's go!

Sun-Kissed Secrets

Secrets hidden in the sand,
A lost flip-flop, isn't it grand?
Seashells wear a grin so wide,
As they listen to crabs' best pride.

Tanned sunbathers with ice cream bliss,
Chasing kids, oh, what a miss!
Sunscreen battles turn quite absurd,
When you find it in a swirly herd.

Starfish gossip by the tide's embrace,
Making up stories about the race.
Under bright skies, we spin and twirl,
As the ocean waves give us a whirl.

With mermaid tales and dolphin tricks,
Each day is filled with silly kicks.
Let's keep dancing in the sun,
In this wacky paradise, we won!

Crystal Waters

Bubbles burst with a giggle,
Fish wear shades, looking regal.
The sea's a comical dance,
Mermaids steal the chance to prance.

Splashing here and splashing there,
Even crabs have time to spare.
Seagulls laugh with a caw and a swoop,
Dancing the day with a fishy loop.

Surfing Serenity

Waves that tumble, float, and tease,
Surfers wobble like a breeze.
The sand shouts, 'Come take a ride!'
While sun hats form a funny slide.

Board shorts flapping in delight,
Tanned folks stumble, what a sight!
A wave crashes, giggles spread,
Even seagulls gasp, 'Enough said!'

Vibrant Vistas

Colors burst like laughter's cheer,
Painted boats all seem to steer.
Palm trees waving, oh so spry,
Dancing to the clouds up high.

Chickens strut with styles so bold,
As beach towels unfold their gold.
Sunglasses perched on noses bright,
Kites flip-flop in the sunlight.

Moonscape by the Shore

The night is bright with a cheeky grin,
Crabs moonwalk, looking for kin.
Stars giggle, twinkle, and glow,
While the tide plays tag, fast and slow.

Balloons drift up, caught by the breeze,
While conch shells chuckle with ease.
Dancers twirl upon the sand,
Caught in the rhythm, hand in hand.

Illuminated Retreat

In flip-flops I sprint, quite a sight,
Sand crabs are fleeing, oh what a fright!
Under umbrellas, I munch and I snack,
Laughter erupts, no worry, no lack.

Seagulls are squawking, trying to steal,
My sandwich and chips, oh the nerve, what a deal!
With shades on my nose, I strike a grand pose,
While sunscreen's a must, it drips, there it goes.

Palm trees are dancing, the breeze is so fine,
I tripped on the beach ball, I'm doing just fine!
Surrounded by giggles, oh isn't it great?
This sunny escape, can't be called fate.

The sun starts to set, I dust off the sand,
With snacks in my hand, I'll make my last stand!
As dolphins do flips, I cheer and I sway,
This laugh-fest retreat, forever I'll stay!

Sunkissed Silhouettes

With drinks made of fruit, I lean on the bar,
My friends all around, we're outshining the stars!
The sun's a delight, we giggle and dance,
As I spill my cocktail, oh what a chance!

Beach towels are flying, like sails in the air,
We dive for the waves, with splashes and flair!
Sandcastle kingdoms, come forth with pride,
Only to find that the tide's on our side.

A seagull named Pete, steals chips from my hand,
With feathers of glory, he thinks he's so grand.
While sunscreen's a fight, that I just can't win,
My left arm's all gleaming, my right's shedding skin!

As nighttime arrives, stars twinkle with glee,
We gather together, just you, snacks and me.
Marshmallows toast while the laughter ignites,
These sunkissed adventures, will bring pure delights!

Radiance of the Distant Wave

I see the sun gleaming, that bright golden glow,
While my towel's a runway, for fashion to show!
With sunglasses on, I'm a model for sure,
If only I could walk without taking a tour!

The tide pulls me in, with a splash and a laugh,
I replenish my drink, it's an orange giraffe!
The fish are all blushing, peeking from their homes,
While I chase a rogue beachball, causing grand combs!

With buckets and shovels, we dig and we play,
I'll build a tall tower before it's decay.
My hat takes a flight, oh where can it land?
It's stuck on a dolphin, too funny to stand!

As shadows grow long, we toast to the sun,
This merriment journey has just begun!
With giggles and joy as our hearts gently wave,
We'll cherish these moments, oh how we behave!

Harboring Daylight

In flip-flops I run, to the shore with a grin,
The tide's at my feet, so let the fun begin!
With laughter that echoes, we jump and we splash,
As sunscreen's our foe, it slips, oh so brash.

The beach ball's insisting on taking a flight,
While sand in my sandwich gives lunch quite a bite.
The sun's on high, it's our stage for the day,
As we dance like the waves, in a comical sway.

The sunset draws near, the horizon aglow,
I'm stung by a jelly, it's not a good show!
But laughter prevails, what a story to share,
With friends all around, there's love in the air.

As stars fill the sky, we reminisce and sing,
Creating stories, oh joy they do bring!
With giggles and light, we'll remember this play,
For harboring sunlight, it's the best kind of day!

Enchanted Tides

Oh, the seaweed danced like a jolly clown,
As waves rolled in with a silly frown.
I tried to surf on a floating shoe,
But ended up tangled, quite like a stew.

The crabs all joined in a conga line,
With a chorus of gulls feeling just fine.
I waved to a fish, it flipped me off,
What a way to make the sea laugh and scoff!

My beach ball flew high, it took a dive,
Into a picnic, oh what a surprise!
Sandwiches scattered, and chips went air-bound,
The laughter around me was all that I found.

As the sun said goodbye, we shared a cheer,
With sea-salt stories and laughter so dear.
I promised the tide, with a wink and a grin,
Next time I'm surfing, I'll make it a win!

Beneath the Azure Skies

Beneath the blue, the seagulls squawk,
I tried to chat, but they just mock.
A fish in a hat swam past my toes,
With a side-eye glance, oh how it shows!

We built a castle, oh what a sight,
The tide rolled in, it gave us a fright.
"Quick, save the moat!" I heard her yell,
As we ran from the wave, what a tale to tell!

Then came the sun with its golden rays,
It melted my ice cream, oh what a craze!
Sandy smiles and a sticky embrace,
Life on the shore is a hilarious race.

At dusk we danced, like fools on the sand,
With jellyfish jigs, hand in hand.
With giggles and splashes, the night took flight,
Oh what fun we had beneath the moonlight!

Sun-kissed Memories

With sunscreen smeared like Picasso's art,
I glided on waves, but fell with a start.
My hat took off in a gusty fuss,
As I chased it down, oh what a plus!

A friendly dolphin jumped and twirled,
While I flopped in the surf, my dreams unfurled.
"I'm a mermaid!" I yelled with a splashy flair,
But just seaweed tangled in my hair!

Frisbee flew high, but landed in glee,
In a stranger's spaghetti, oh can't you see?
We laughed and shared bites of our meals,
As the sun dipped low, revealing squeals.

As night fell, we passed stories around,
About beach blunders, oh the laughter found.
With salt-kissed breezes and smiles so wide,
We made sun-filled memories that never hide!

Driftwood Ballad

On the shore where driftwood sings a tune,
I found a crab playing the spoons.
With laughter echoing in the salty air,
We danced on the beach without a care.

A flip-flop pirate sailed on the sand,
With treasure made of shells in his hand.
He traded me tales for a jellybean,
Together we laughed until we turned green.

I tried to catch a wave on a slice of bread,
But wound up tumbling, almost dead!
The seagulls swooped down, stole my treat,
They flapped their wings to the beat of my defeat.

As sunset painted the sky with glee,
We sang a song for the sea to see.
Driftwood dreams and quirky fun,
In this coastal ballad, we are never done!

Harbor of Dreams

In a place where seagulls squawk,
And crabs dance in a silly walk,
The boats tiptoe on the bay,
While fish gossip about their day.

A lighthouse with a comical grin,
Winks at the waves, let the fun begin!
Shells play hide and seek with the sand,
While the sun shines on this merry land.

Here dolphins wear their party hats,
Balloons float by on friendly chats,
The sandcastles throw a dance-off,
Where builders cheer and nobody scoffs.

So come on down, don't be shy,
The waves want to teach you to fly,
With popcorn skies and jellybean dreams,
Life's a laugh, or so it seems!

The Symphony of Echoes

Whispers bounce from tree to tree,
As monkeys practice their harmony,
The ocean claps with a splashy cheer,
While the wind giggles, drawing near.

A crab conducts with a sneaky claw,
Creating music that leaves us in awe,
Clams hum low, while the gulls sing high,
It's a concert that tickles the sky.

The waves joke around and paint the shore,
With stories of pirates and treasure galore,
Each echo we hear is a laugh in disguise,
As the dolphins dance beneath sunlit skies.

So tap your feet to the tidal beat,
For this orchestra's not quite discreet,
Join in the fun, don't be late,
This symphony aims to generate laughter's fate!

Radiant Blue

The sea is a canvas, a merry hue,
With splashes of sunshine and frolicking crew,
The fish wear bowties, looking quite smart,
While seaweed sways like it's doing its part.

A buoy dances, full of delight,
Sings sea shanties all through the night,
While crabs juggle shells in a flashy display,
And waves throw a party, come join the play!

The ocean floor has a comedic flair,
With starfish rolling like they haven't a care,
Turtles in sunglasses strut down the lane,
While otters engage in aquatic champagne.

So come for a splash, stay for the glee,
In shades of blue, wild and free,
It's a watery palace of giggles and cheer,
Where laughter floats, and hearts draw near!

Resplendent Refuge

In a nook where laughter meets the shore,
The crickets chirp and the sea gulls roar,
There's a tree that tickles the clouds above,
A whimsical place, brimming with love.

Sandy toes and flip-flop dance moves,
Seashells giggle with their shiny grooves,
The sunbeams join in with rhythm and cheer,
Making memories as we all draw near.

Benches made from driftwood dreams,
Where the giggles float on gossamer beams,
Coconuts serve as the drink of the day,
While the breeze carries worries far away.

So grab your friends, let's make a toast,
To laughter and sunsets we'll love the most,
In this haven of joy, forever we'll stay,
In this delightful retreat where we play!

Waves of Serenity

The ocean laughed, a bubbly tease,
Seagulls danced with the flapping breeze.
Crabs in bow ties strutted with flair,
Turtles in shades lounged without a care.

Surfboards flipped like pancakes on sand,
While the octopus built castles so grand.
Jellyfish joined in a wobbly show,
As fishes revved up in a school below.

Mermaids giggled at the splashy scene,
Dolphins wore hats, oh so pristine.
Lemonade waves in coconut cups,
Tides of laughter, nobody hurries up.

Sandy toes and sunscreen's a mess,
Finding a crab was anyone's guess.
Sunsets painted with ice cream streaks,
As nighttime brought in the starry peaks.

Whispers of the Nautilus

In a shell with secrets, whispers take flight,
A clam tried to sing, but got wrapped up tight.
Starfish gossip on the warm ocean floor,
While lobsters get fancy, with cabaret lore.

Turtles tell tales of their weekend quests,
Where fish wear pajamas and all take their rests.
Shrimps join a band, with sand as their stage,
Bubbles and laughter, just the right gauge.

A sable sea horse, slick with pride,
Chased after bubbles like a joyride.
Seashells exchanged stories in morning's embrace,
As a seagull lost its sunglasses in haste.

With every flip of the wave and swell,
The humor in ocean's hilarious spell.
Laughter echoes through the water's sway,
Where the cods wear wigs, just for play!

Gaze upon the Horizon

Gazing far where the sky takes a dive,
A crab in a bowler hat, feeling alive.
Sailing boats with squirrels at the wheel,
Chia pets bobbing, oh what a deal!

Dolphins with disco moves left and right,
Flipping and flopping, oh what a sight!
Pelicans fashionably late for the ball,
While turtles on surfboards just munch and sprawl.

Rays of sunshine grin, a cheeky smile,
While fish flaunt their sparkles, going a mile.
Salty breezes whisper sweet jokes of delight,
The horizon's a canvas – oh, what a sight!

A wave full of giggles, a splash of bright fun,
With bubbles of laughter, dance in the sun.
Seashells collect secrets, tales to tell,
In this quirky paradise, all is well.

The Mellow Sea

The mellow sea, it hums a tune,
As crabs read poems under the moon.
Dolphins wear shades, cool as can be,
And starfish try yoga, so wild and free.

A fish in a top hat charades on a wave,
While octopuses juggle, oh how they behave!
Lobsters knitting sweaters, just for the thrill,
All while the water drinks up the chill.

Sandy shores host a party so grand,
With seashells as guests, aren't they just dandy?
The breeze sways softly, inviting a joke,
As pelicans swoop down, not a word they spoke.

Sunsets pour colors like sweet lemonade,
With laughter and joy in the warmth's cascade.
The mellow sea chuckles, waves breaking free,
A blend of bright humor, pure jubilee!

Moonlit Mariner's Song

Oh, the moon's a shiny coin,
Bobbing on the waves so fine.
Sailing boats with squeaky sails,
Fish are dancing, telling tales.

Coconuts in captain's hats,
Pirates laugh, and that's a fact!
Stars above, they wink and gleam,
Whispering secrets in your dream.

Seagulls sing in off-key notes,
While the boats do silly floats.
Catch a crab, it gives a wave,
He's the star of this sea rave.

So hoist the sails and let them sway,
Join the fun, don't miss the play!
Through the night, we'll shimmy, shake,
Living free, for laughter's sake.

Celestial Currents

The sky is painted, orange and blue,
Nautical nonsense in our view.
Octopus playing tambourine,
The silliest band we've ever seen.

Mermaids giggle as they splash,
Doing belly flops with a crash.
Crab walks by like he's the boss,
With a swagger, he'll never toss.

Jellyfish dance with polka dots,
Time to tie some funny knots.
Watch out now, a wave of foam,
Here come the fish, just like a gnome!

Underneath the twinkling lights,
We'll joke and jibe through starry nights.
With laughter sailing through the air,
Join the fun, there's joy to share!

Warm Embraces of the Sea

Breezy laughter on the shore,
Beach balls bouncing, oh, what a score!
Sunscreen applied with a funny face,
Sticky hands in a wild embrace.

Seashells whisper, secrets found,
As the waves crash with a sound.
Turtles groove in their own way,
Hitting the dance floor, come what may.

Flip-flops flip and flops will fly,
Breezes bring a silly sigh.
Waves lapping at our feet with glee,
Sprinkling joy, that's the key!

Jumping in with shouts and cheer,
Making the ocean our frontier.
So let's enjoy this sea-spun play,
In the sun, we'll laugh and sway!

Ebb and Flow of Golden Light

Golden beams on day's fresh start,
Tickling toes and warming hearts.
Sandcastles built with formless dreams,
A kingdom ruled by silly schemes.

Waves come crashing in a swirl,
A fishy dance, a wiggly twirl.
Hermit crabs in tiny suits,
Strutting up in fancy boots.

Napping dolphins on a raft,
Telling tales and sharing a laugh.
The sun is bright, the sky's a show,
Chasing shadows, let's all go!

As the tides of joy parade,
We'll indulge in this sunlit charade.
So gather 'round, let mirth ignite,
In the merry ebb and golden light!

Elysium's Touch

In a land where coconuts fall,
I slipped on a peel, what a sprawl!
Crabs dance around, they think it's a show,
While I juggle fruits, putting on a glow.

Chasing seagulls, I try to impress,
They steal my snacks, oh what a mess!
I dive for a treasure that's shiny and bright,
Turns out it's just a bottle—oh what a fright!

The sun loves to roast me, a big silly grin,
As I wear my hat like a crown of a king.
Fish peek and giggle, oh what a delight,
In this wacky world where humor takes flight.

With waves that sing tales of laughter and cheer,
Every bump on the boat makes jokes disappear.
So toast to the goofballs who dance with the breeze,
In this paradise, nothing's serious, please!

The Promise of Sand and Sun

In the morning, my sandwich took flight,
Its crust a strange kite, what a sight!
Pelicans squawk, they steal with glee,
While I chase my lunch, oh woe is me!

Sandcastles crumble like dreams gone awry,
As toddlers stampede, oh me, oh my!
I built a fort fit for a king,
But a wave came along and stole everything.

A hermit crab waves, a curious guest,
He claps his claws, putting me to rest.
I laugh at his dance, it's quite the affair,
In the sun's warm embrace, we make quite the pair.

As twilight approaches, the fireflies stir,
I trip on my flip-flops, oh what a blur!
But laughter erupts, like bubbles in soda,
In this sandy retreat, joy can't be colder!

Horizon's Glow

Walking a tightrope of seaweed and brine,
I nearly fall over, oh isn't life fine?
A dolphin pokes fun, flips high in the air,
While I splash around like I haven't a care.

The sun sets low, painting skies with a grin,
As I sport my best tan, looking quite thin.
Seagulls squawk jokes that they think I should hear,
While I try not to trip over my own two feet here.

A treasure map drawn in the sand with a stick,
Leads me to candy—oh what a quick pick!
But ants march along, claiming their prize,
I join their parade and we all harmonize.

So here's to the laughter, the silliness, too,
In this playful realm where dreams come unglued!
With friends far and wide, and fun all around,
We revel together, where joy knows no bound!

The Embrace of the Water

I waddle with grace, like a duck on the shore,
While mermaids giggle, they want to explore.
I brought a rubber duck for a swim,
Turns out it quacked back—oh how it did grin!

Coconut drinks that I spill on my shirt,
The locals just chuckle, it's all in good hurt.
A parrot helps me with tips on the best,
But I think it's just trying to prank my quest.

With waves that tease and gently caress,
I tumble and roll, oh what a mess!
But laughter ignites, and that's the real prize,
In this silly haven, where joy multiplies.

So let's dance with the tides, sing songs to the moon,
In this world of folly, may we never feel gloom!
As we float on our backs, counting stars one by one,
I tip my hat to the night, and say, 'Isn't this fun?'

Dawn's Tender Touch

The sun stretches, yawns, and grins,
As sleepy birds play hide and seek.
A crab does a jig, his dance begins,
While turtles moan, 'We need more sleep!'

The waves chuckle with each embrace,
A starfish rolls, 'I'm feeling bold!'
Seagulls shout, 'Oh, what a place!'
While shells gossip tales of old.

A lone coconut might just fall,
On unsuspecting heads it lands.
With laughter echoing through it all,
Nature's rumor mill expands!

What joy in this bright, silly show,
Where sun and sea play all day long.
The world shines in a funny glow,
A melody of life, a cheerful song.

Nature's Sunlit Canvas

The sky paints itself in shades of blue,
With splashes of clouds that float around.
A dolphin leaps, just passing through,
While beachcombers laugh at the found.

Bananas wear hats, they look quite chic,
As crabs in bow ties strut with flair.
The breeze gives a tickle, it's quite unique,
While children squeal, trailing everywhere.

A jellyfish jiggles, making waves,
While sandcastles rise in a clumsy fashion.
The ocean's whispers, a symphony saves,
Bringing laughter and silly, carefree passion.

Colors dance in the sun's bright light,
Each hue a step in the morning waltz.
Nature's gallery, a cheeky delight,
Turns every mishap into a vault!

Warm Breeze and Bright Skies

A warm breeze tickles the palm fronds high,
As flip-flops flop on sandy trails.
With every gust, kites start to fly,
While a crab says, 'Life never fails!'

The sun's a clown, it brightens the day,
While seashells wink with little glee.
A pig on the shore rolls in hay,
Declaring, 'I'm the best as can be!'

Parrots squawk, 'Let's dance the night!'
While fish gossip in glittery schools.
This vibrant realm feels just so right,
Where dancing critters break the rules.

Clouds wear shades, they chill and prep,
Nature's comedy, no time to stress.
As laughter flows, we take a step,
On vibrant paths toward happiness!

Colors of the Tide

The tide rolls in, a painter's spree,
With brushes made of sails and foam.
Crabs and seagulls, such jolly glee,
They waddle and squawk—this is home!

A beach ball dreams of grander heights,
While surfboards chat about their plans.
Behind it all, the sun ignites,
As starfish whisper, 'Hey, I'm a fan!'

The ocean's laughter ripples wide,
While waves crash down in playful mood.
With every splash, the colors glide,
Creating joy, oh-so-very good!

Nature's hues are bold and bright,
In this spectacle we adore.
Every detail, a thrilling sight,
Where color and charm forever soar!

Eternal Vistas

Beneath the sun's bright winks, they prance,
A group of tourists caught in dance.
Sunglasses on, they strike a pose,
While seagulls plot to steal their clothes.

The sandy stretch becomes a stage,
With surfboards clashing, oh what a rage!
Yet in this folly, laughter swells,
As clumsy surfers swap their shells.

A crab with swagger walks the line,
It scoffs at humans chasing sunshine.
Yet all admire its little strut,
While sunburns form a goofy glut.

At dusk, they toast with fruity blends,
And share their tales with newfound friends.
What fun it is to roam and roam,
In places that feel just like home.

Tidal Serenade

The waves do dance in joyful glee,
A fish dips low, can't you see?
It flops and flails, puts on a show,
While sunburnt dudes just move too slow.

Seashells gossip on the shore,
Whispering tales of ocean lore.
A starfish giggles, it seems to know,
That life's a joke, just let it flow.

As footprints fade like silly dreams,
Waves crash on the sand with gleams.
Each splash erupts in fits of glee,
A hilarious underwater spree.

When night descends, they play charades,
With crickets chirping, it serenades.
A playful night under starry rays,
As laughter echoes, it always stays.

Cascade of Colors

The sunset spills its paint on skies,
Like jelly beans before your eyes.
Palm trees sway in silly grins,
While piña coladas drown their sins.

A parrot squawks with tongue-in-cheek,
It squabbles with a dolphin, sleek.
They argue who is cooler still,
While kids run wild, their spirits thrill.

Berry-colored drinks in hand,
The grown-ups dream of mock bands.
Yet in this madness, joy prevails,
As laughter rides the breezy gales.

The night unveils its twinkling lights,
As everyone shares peculiar sights.
In this vivid, tropical chaos,
Life's a joke, and it's really boss!

A Sanctuary of Light

The sun peeks in, oh what a sight,
Illuminating every delight.
Sandy toes dance in the air,
As flip-flops fly without a care.

Bikini blunders and sun-worn frowns,
Make for giggles in bustling towns.
And every laugh is music made,
As sunscreen battles the sun's parade.

In this warm and cheery haven,
A turtle sings, his shell is craven.
He steals the spotlight for a while,
With every quirky, slow-motion smile.

Beneath a sky of pastel hues,
They wonder what they'll laugh about next news.
A sanctuary where joy is light,
With jokes and jests, it feels just right.

Echoes of the Tides

A crab wore a hat, oh so bright,
Strutting his stuff, what a sight!
He danced on the sand, quite the show,
While seagulls squawked, 'Hey, take it slow!'

The waves gave a chuckle, a splashy cheer,
As fish flipped their tails like they had no fear!
Starfish played cards, with shells as their chips,
Laughing so hard, they fell off their lips.

A dolphin joked, 'I'm the king of the sea!'
While the octopus winked, 'Maybe just a bee!'
They swam in circles, in giggly delight,
While the beachgoers all took flight.

So if you hear laughter, over the foam,
Just know that the ocean has made it its home!
Adventures await, with joy and with glee,
In the world where the silly fish swim free!

Nautical Dreams

A pirate so bold, lost his treasure map,
Instead, he found a funny cat nap!
He slept through the storms, through thunder and rain,
While his crew sang songs, again and again.

The gulls wore mustaches, oh what a sight,
Squawking in rhymes, such a comical plight!
A fish called a meeting, said 'Let's go swim!'
But the crabs brought snacks, so the chance grew dim.

A mermaid blew bubbles, with laughter and cheer,
'Catch me if you can', she said with a sneer!
But really, they all just wanted to play,
In dreams of the sea, they'd stay night and day.

So here's to the sailors, the ones with the jokes,
Who swap out their anchors for ticklish strokes!
The ocean's their stage, where laughter's supreme,
Living out wild, nautical dreams!

Radiant Horizons

Beneath a sun wearing sunglasses so wide,
The sunbathers giggled in a tandem glide.
They built the sandcastles, tall and so grand,
But seagulls conspired, they plotted and planned!

With a swoop and a flap, they stole all the fries,
While the kids just stared with wide-open eyes.
'Hey! Those are ours!' cried a boy with a grin,
As the gulls laughed out loud, and made their escape win!

The crabs joined the crowd, in the snack-stealing fun,
Dancing like crazy, oh what a run!
While wise old turtles, in slow-motion stunts,
Shook their heads sadly, calling them brunts!

So grab your sunscreen, let's all join the play,
For each silly moment, come seize the day!
With laughter like sunshine, splashing so bright,
We'll cherish these rays all through the night!

Luminous Shores

Dolphins in top hats, what a sight to behold!
Waltzing on waves like they'd grown so bold.
With each flip and splash, they shone like new,
While fish rolled their eyes, 'This just won't do!'

The wise old octopus, with eight arms to spare,
Juggled beach balls, as kids stopped to stare.
He tripped on a starfish, fell right on his face,
The beach erupted in giggles, such a funny place!

A pelican wobbled, with a hat on his beak,
As he tried to dance, but his footing was weak.
With shells as his shoes, he gave it a whirl,
And soon all the crabs joined in with a twirl!

So if you're near shores, where laughter does play,
Just know that the creatures bring joy every day!
With humour and fun, like the sun's golden rays,
The ocean's a dreamland, in so many ways!

Shimmering Shores

On the sand, a crab dances and prances,
Waving its claws in silly romances.
Seagulls squawk with a playful cheer,
While sunbathers hide—oh dear, oh dear!

Beach balls bounce with a jolly sound,
As toddlers tumble and roll all around.
The waves come in like a playful pup,
But careful now, don't spill your cup!

Sunscreen's splattered like abstract art,
Rubbed on folks who haven't a good start.
Flip-flops flapping in the bright, warm air,
Yo-yos whirling without a care!

As whispers of seaweed float and intertwine,
A beach party croaks like an off-key line.
With laughter and sprinkles of salt in the breeze,
These are the moments that bring us to our knees!

Shores of Existence

Beneath the sun, a porpoise leaps,
While tourists spill their icy keeps.
Sandcastles wobble, a royal scene,
As a kid screams loud, 'Hey, look at my queen!'

In the distance, a beach ball flies,
Hitting a man with cucumber eyes.
The ocean chuckles, waves do their thing,
As floaties wear crowns, like the new king.

Sunglasses slide down noses with grace,
As a doggie digs up a sandy place.
Everyone's sun-kissed, with giggles galore,
With a crab leading the conga on the shore!

The cool tide rolls, like a dance of the sea,
And surprises await, oh what can they be?
In the quirky embrace of the surf's crazy dance,
We find joy in giggles and the luck of chance!

Secrets Beneath the Surface

Beneath the waves, a crab in shades,
Trying to dance but never parades.
Seagulls laugh at his frantic moves,
While fish snicker in slick grooves.

A lobster dreams of disco balls,
In a treasure chest with no more walls.
He invites a shrimp to join the fun,
But all they do is catch the sun.

A whale practices its opera song,
While a clam hums along, right or wrong.
Under the sea, it's quite a spree,
With bubbles of laughter, wild and free.

Sunkissed Alleys

In sunny lanes where shadows dance,
The cats wear shades and take a chance.
They strut like models down the block,
While pigeons gossip 'round the clock.

A gelato stand starts a sweet race,
With sprinkles flying all over the place.
Kids giggle, chasing after a drip,
In this wild, wacky summer trip.

Lizards lounge, pretending to sun,
Their tiny hearts beat just for fun.
With sunglasses on, they sidestep the heat,
Savoring each tiny, crunchy treat.

The Solstice Tide

The waves roll in with an unfunny joke,
While surfers fall like a silly folk.
They paddle hard, but the swell's too grand,
With every wipeout, they wave their hands.

A sandcastle king sits tall and proud,
Until a seagull lands, all loud.
Down it goes with a single peck,
"Who needs a palace? I'll go wreck!"

Flip-flops flip on the sandy shore,
In pirouettes they never implore.
Each step a giggle, a jolly blunder,
As they dance with joy beneath the thunder.

Fleeting Moments by the Sea

A starfish flips with a jolly grin,
Says, "Come join me, let the fun begin!"
The tide rolls in with a big belly laugh,
And dolphins plot their next goofy gaffe.

A crab wearing shades digs for gold,
While the clams hide stories, shy and old.
With every splash, there's a new surprise,
As seagulls play tag in the sunny skies.

A beach ball bounces, heads dart and sway,
While everyone laughs at a dog's splay.
Chasing waves, they run with glee,
Capturing moments, forever carefree.

Tranquil Reflections of Light

The sun got lost in the ocean's grin,
Chasing shadows where the waves begin.
A flip-flop floats on a jellyfish ride,
While seagulls argue, oh what a tide!

A starfish sticks to its rock so tight,
Pondering life under soft sunlight.
Crabs hold meetings, with claws held high,
Planning a party, oh me, oh my!

Wet towels hanging like laundry bright,
Someone's sunscreen is now out of sight!
Beach balls tumble with boisterous glee,
As sand gets in my drink—oh, whee!

But laughter rings where the waves break loose,
Funny tales carried on waves of juice.
Who knew sunlight could be such a jest?
Tranquil reflections at their best!

Dance of Sun and Sea

The surf is dancing with a cheeky swish,
While dolphins leap, oh what a wish!
A piña colada spills, laughter does soar,
As flip-flops fling—right to the shore!

Seashells whisper secrets, oh so grand,
While children build castles from seaweed sand.
A crab in a tutu struts down the line,
Sassy and festive, feeling divine!

The breeze brings gossip from tropical trees,
And sunburned tourists beg for a freeze.
Each splash and giggle a rhythmic refrain,
In the dance where sunshine and waves entertain!

So grab a coconut, come join the spree,
Where the sun meets the sea so merrily.
Let's twirl with the tide, in a whirl of delight,
In this funny dance of morning to night!

Shores of Solitude

On these shores, silence wears a huge hat,
Yet whispers of crabs sound more like a chat.
A lone beach towel, sunbaked and bold,
Remembers tales of sunscreen gone old.

The ocean's laughter bubbles and rolls,
As seagulls play games with our sandwich rolls.
Each wave a punchline, a splashy surprise,
Where fish teach humor right before our eyes!

A sailor's hat floats, without a care,
While pelicans plot to steal the fair share.
The sun beamed down an unwritten script,
But sand fills my shoes—what a funny trip!

In solitude's calm, there's humor to spare,
A funny little world, without a care.
With jesters in shells, eternally free,
This shore transcends, such creativity!

Sunlit Whispers

Soft whispers of warmth on a playful breeze,
Flip-flops gossip about old-time stories.
The sun's bright chuckle tickles the sea,
While turtles wiggle with cheeky glee!

A fishing pole bent like a llama's neck,
And seaweed wigs make quite the deck.
As laughter carries on air so sweet,
Every grain of sand is light on our feet!

Seashells collect secrets, chuckling low,
While crabs put on their grand comedy show.
Coconut drinks, oh, aren't they divine?
In a world of fun, we sip and recline!

So raise a toast to this golden affair,
With sunlit whispers, let's shed every care.
Where laughter paints colors across the blue,
In this cheerful paradise, just me and you!

Celestial Coastlines

On sandy shores, a crab did dance,
Wiggling legs in a clumsy prance.
A seagull squawked, a fishy jest,
As beachgoers laughed, forgot their rest.

A sunburned man, a hat askew,
Chased a seagull who slyly flew.
Losing his flip-flops in the chase,
He tripped on sand, what a funny face!

Turtles surfed on swells of blue,
While kids built castles without a clue.
A wave crashed down, and oh, what a sight,
Their dreams went splash in sheer delight!

As twilight settled, laughter echoed near,
A dolphin danced, bringing them cheer.
With pies in the sky and stars so bright,
The coast was alive, a joy-filled night.

Kaleidoscope of Waves

A jellyfish wore a funky hat,
With polka dots, imagine that!
It floated by, in gentle sway,
While children giggled and splashed all day.

A surfboard tried to catch a breeze,
But tripped on waves with all its ease.
Its rider soared, then lost the fight,
Turning a flip, oh, what a sight!

Umbrellas flipped with drunken grace,
As winds played tag, what a mad race!
Chasing piña coladas, oh so sweet,
Running for shade on their sandy feet!

At twilight's call, the laughter grew,
As crabs in tuxedos danced in view.
A masterpiece of silly fun,
In this swirl of colors, joy had won.

Golden Dusk

A beach ball bounced from kid to kid,
A puppy chased it, with a skid.
Sandcastles crumbled with every toss,
As laughter echoed, no one felt loss.

The sun began to dip real low,
While waves whispered tales of woe.
A seagull swooped, and chips were shared,
With crumbs of joy, kids never cared.

Sunburned noses, red as could be,
The ice cream truck called out with glee.
Flavors like bubblegum and mint,
Had everyone laughing, not a hint!

As night drew in, the bonfire glowed,
With storytelling and laughter flowed.
Starry skies above, moon's bright smile,
Time to be silly, at least for a while!

Harmony of the Harmonious Waves

A hermit crab played a tiny flute,
While a fish danced, oh, how cute!
The tide rolled in, bringing the beat,
As seaweed swayed, moving their feet.

Seashells clinked in funky rhythm,
Crab playing solo, he had the wisdom.
Clownfish chuckled, their colors bright,
Swirling around in pure delight.

A turtle tripped on a sunken shoe,
Flipped on its back, but had a view.
With shouts and giggles, it rolled and spun,
A grand performance, oh what fun!

The sun dipped low, paintbrush sky,
"Let's make a toast!" a walrus cried.
With clam cocktails and laughter uncorked,
Together they danced, a joy-filled court!

Secrets of the Coastal Breeze

The seagulls squawk in stylish flight,
While crabs hold court, oh what a sight!
Beach towels flutter like flags so proud,
As folks trip over their snacks, unbowed.

The sunbathers nap with ice cream dreams,
While sunscreen battles a slip 'n' slide theme.
A kid builds castles, but wait — oh no!
A wave crashes down, and he bursts in woe!

A picnic spread with chips galore,
But ants have joined the party for sure!
The laughter echoes, tunes out the fuss,
As someone yells, "Who packed this mess?"

With every breeze, mischief takes flight,
And sand gets everywhere, oh what a sight!
Yet smiles abound on this coastal spree,
For who can frown when they're wild and free?

The Call of Distant Waters

Far-off waves chant a silly song,
While fish throw parties, all night long.
Turtles in shades lounge on the shore,
While mermaids giggle, begging for more!

A sailor yells, "Ahoy, let's play!"
But gets lost in knots — oh what dismay!
His compass spins like a dizzy thrill,
For every sea breeze brings a new spill.

Bubbles rise, and laughter spreads,
As seaweed wigs dance on vacation heads.
The gulls pull pranks, swooping with grace,
Stealing hats right off folks' face!

Yet every splash brings giggles galore,
As muddy toes track in the door!
So here's to the whimsy of ocean's call,
Where fun's the rule, and we joyfully fall!

Glistening Sands

Golden grains whisper in the sun,
While sunscreen looking like a gooey run!
Flip-flops flying, oh what a chase,
As kids do the cha-cha with mud on their face!

A sandcastle topped with seashell flair,
But a toddler's hand claims it, unaware.
"Look at me, I'm a beachy king!"
Until the tide comes and makes it a fling!

Umbrellas dance like worried bugs,
As wind snatches drinks with sneaky hugs.
Laughter erupts when a wave comes crashing,
And everyone's diving; it's quite the thrashing!

Yet still on these shores where fun collides,
Miracles happen with laughter as guides.
In salty air and cool, breezy nights,
Every giggle shines, oh what pure delights!

Hidden Havens

In cozy nooks where laughter swells,
Tropical drinks in bright, funny shells.
Beach bums debate like pros at a test,
"Is it sunset or sunrise? We're so blessed!"

Shy crabs peek from their secret dens,
While seagulls snagging fries are fierce little friends.
A hammock swings with a wobbly zest,
As someone yells, "I need a rest!"

With coconuts rolling on sandy floors,
A squirrel plays pirate; behold the uproar!
The laughter bubbles like a fizzy drink,
As pals exchange jokes and food with a wink.

So here in the haven where silliness reigns,
With sunshine spilling like rivers of gains,
We find sweet joy in every bright quirk,
In laughter and love, we deeply smirk.

www.ingramcontent.com/pod-product-compliance
Lightning Source LLC
Chambersburg PA
CBHW072131070526
44585CB00016B/1619